Motoring Law Handbook

Motoring Law Handbook
by Felicity Mileham

Published by
Law Pack Publishing Limited
10-16 Cole Street
London SE1 4YH
www.lawpack.co.uk

Printed in Great Britain

ISBN: 1 902646 35 5

Important facts

Welcome to this Law Pack Motoring Law Handbook. It is packed with useful information and advice on your rights as a motorist. However please note the following.

This Handbook is intended for use in England and Wales. However, much of the legislation is generally applicable, or is mirrored, in Scotland and Northern Ireland, but readers are advised that procedures vary in these jurisdictions.

The information this Handbook contains has been carefully compiled from professional sources, but its accuracy cannot be guaranteed, as laws and regulations may change or be subject to differing interpretations.

Neither this nor any other publication can take the place of a solicitor on important legal matters. As with any legal matter, common sense should determine whether you need the assistance of a solicitor rather than relying solely on the information in this Law Pack Handbook.

Exclusion of Liability and Disclaimer

Contents

Introduction

Motoring law affects us all. This is particularly so for drivers and motorcycle owners, but it is also true for pedestrians and other road users. Every time we get into a car there are implications in criminal law (the panoply of road traffic offences) and in civil law (our duty to take care for the safety of other road users). Buying a vehicle involves us in the law of contract amongst other things and driving abroad brings us into contact with the law of foreign countries.

This Handbook is intended to provide an overview of each of these things and other areas of motoring law for the motorist. The emphasis is on practical advice, rather than than in-depth analysis of the substantive law. Where matters are too serious or complex to be dealt with by a general guide such as this, you are warned to take legal advice. However, with the help of this Handbook it is hoped you will become aware of your rights as a motorist, and will be able to deal with the Courts with confidence. Happy motoring!

Felicity Mileham

Mitre Court Chambers, London

Chapter 1

The garage

Purchasing a vehicle

When you buy a car (or bicycle or motorbike) or have one repaired the deal between you and the seller or garage is governed by the law of contract, a branch of the civil law. Of course, if a seller has acted in bad faith or unlawfully there may also be other legal consequences (e.g. a crime may have been committed, or Trading Standards infringed). This chapter, however, concentrates on how to avoid the pitfalls when dealing with the garage or private seller, and describes what you can claim for if things have gone wrong. Whilst the chapter refers to buying cars, the principles apply also to the purchase of bicycles, motor bicycles and other vehicles.

Buying a new car

If you are buying a new car you will be dealing with a dealer (i.e. a person or company whose business it is to sell cars), and the chances are that the contract will be a written one, and probably will include a warranty, and package of other benefits.

Buying a used car

You might purchase a used car from a dealer or from a private individual, in which case the contract may be written, oral or both. The protection given to you by the law is different in each of these cases and are discussed below. However, the fundamental principle remains: that you can sue the seller if there has been 'breach of contract' or if he/she has 'misrepresented' a material fact which had induced you to buy the car. Misrepresentation is dealt with separately below. Finally, a word of warning, this Guide deals solely with the legal position in dealing with the garage, only mentioning in passing how you can safeguard yourself against buying an expensive and troublesome dud. There are many specialist books available which give advice on what mechanical defects and 'tricks of the trade' to look out for, as well as market prices guidelines. These should be referred to in order to avoid ever having to call upon the law!

Breach of contract : buying from a dealer

As long as you are a private consumer the Sale of Goods Act 1979 (as amended) offers you some protection. This is because the Act demands that cars (or bicycles and motor bicycles) sold to private consumers by dealers must be of 'satisfactory quality'. This is a question of fact, and the Courts will take account of the price paid, the make, age and model, and any other relevant factors. The Act also requires that a car sold to a consumer must also be reasonably fit for a purpose made known to the seller by the buyer. Usually the buyer will by implication require a car that can be driven along a road for a reasonable mileage and period after the purchase. Thus if the car becomes undriveable shortly after it was bought you may have a claim against the seller. If you told the garage that you wanted the car for a specific purpose and the car turns out to be unfit for that purpose you may also have a claim.

Breach of contract: buying from a private seller

When you buy a car (bicycle or motorbike) from someone who does not sell cars for a living there is no protection from the Sale of Goods Act. Basically, 'buyer beware!'. This means it is up to you to ensure that there are no defects before you buy. You are unlikely to be able to sue the seller for defects that become apparent after the sale, and the best advice is to ensure that you know as much as possible about the vehicle, its condition and history, before you hand over any money.

Warning!

If the seller draws your attention to a defect before you buy the car, you will not be able to complain about it at a later date. Similarly, if you have had a chance to examine the car before purchasing and fail to spot or decide to ignore a defect should have been apparent to you, you will not be able to sue in respect of that defect. This might occur, for example, if the door handle was broken.

Quite simply, you get what you pay for. What may be an unacceptable fault in a new or nearly-new car may not be (legally) unacceptable in an elderly car of large mileage which you bought at a comparatively low market price. The older the car the more problems it is likely to get and the courts will take this into account.

Misrepresentation

If the vehicle does not match up to the description or promises made by the seller (either a dealer or an individual) before the deal was struck, you may be able to claim for 'misrepresentation', (whether or not the seller acted in good faith). Note also that only statements of fact, rather than opinions or law can amount to a misrepresentation.

If there has been a misrepresentation you are entitled either to your money back (and return of the car to the previous owner), or to a sum representing the difference in value between the value of the car you contracted to buy and the value of the car that you actually got. If you wish to return the car and obtain a refund of the money you paid out you must act quickly. Often, where the purchaser has delayed returning the car (or telling the seller to come and pick it up), or a long time has passed since the contract was formed the courts will simply award the buyer damages (in practice, a smaller sum than the purchase price). Of course, your other option is to report the matter to Trading Standards who may prosecute the seller. A successful conviction of the seller may result in you being awarded compensation by the court.

> *Example:*
> Miss A tells Mr B that the car she wants to sell has a mileage of 60,000. Mr B likes the car and partly relying on the fact that the car only has 60,000 on the clock agrees to buy. It transpires that the car has been 'clocked' and the true mileage is 120,000 miles. Mr B has a claim for misrepresentation against Miss A.

Stolen vehicles

If you buy a vehicle that subsequently turns out to have been stolen you have no rights over it as it still belongs to the original owner (or the insurance company).

Your only claim is against the person who sold it to you, which may be difficult in practice. If the seller is convicted of theft, or a related crime in respect of the car, the court may award you compensation, but this is unlikely to get you all your money back. To guard against this unfortunate position it is sensible to do a check on the vehicle before you buy. Equifax is an organisation which will search a database to see if the car you intend to buy has been reported stolen, 'written off' by the insurers or still subject to a Hire Purchase agreement. Equifax can be contacted on telephone 01722 413434. You will be charged a fee for this service, currently £31.00.

'Ringing' and 'clocking'

Unscrupulous sellers may have given a stolen car a new identity by swapping the registration plates, obtaining replacement paperwork from the DVLA and re-engraving the chassis and engine numbers. This is known as 'ringing'. To lessen the risk of buying such a car obtain an Equifax check by telephone. This may reveal the car to be a write-off or stolen. Otherwise keep an eye out for physical marks of an altered identity. 'Clocking' is the illegal practice of winding back the mileometer to show a lesser mileage. There may be visible signs of the fascia being forced (scratched plastic) or signals that the car may have been much more used than the mileage suggests (i.e. a higher than expected degree of wear and tear).

Repairing a vehicle

When you take your car into a garage, both you and the garage have contractual responsibilities to fulfil, and the contract is governed by the Supply of Goods and Services Act 1982. The work you have asked them to do must be done with 'reasonable skill and care' - shoddy workmanship is a breach of the contract. However, under the contract you must pay the price agreed. The garage may lawfully refuse to release your car until the fees are paid. This is known as 'exercising a lien' over your property. Of course most defects are not immediately apparent and will only be detected after you have paid the garage on removing your car, so in practice this situation will rarely arise.

If you are unhappy about the service you have been given you should pay the sum required, and obtain a report from another engineer analysing the condition of the car and stating whether the service provided was up to standard or not. If you are successful in proving the garage did not provide the appropriate standard of service, the cost of such an expert report, together with other legal costs will normally be recoverable. Note that if you cancel a cheque the garage may sue you for the money on the dishonoured cheque, and if it does you will be ordered to pay the amount under an obscure rule of law known as the 'cheque rule'. You will then have to bring a separate claim for your money back on the basis of the garage's breach of contract.

Practical steps

The first step is to offer the seller or garage, whether a company, individual car dealer or private person, the opportunity of putting matters right. If there has been a substantial breach of contract (e.g. major repairs or replacement of parts needed) or if there has been a misrepresentation, and you do not want to keep the car, write to the seller at once stating that you want to return the car. You should tell him or her to arrange to pick up the car, and do not use it further. If you paid for the car in instalments do not pay any more. Instead ask the seller to return the money you have already paid to him. If this does not work send a 'letter before action' which asks him to return your money and collect the car within a certain time and warns him that if he does not do so you will take him to court.

If you are happy to keep the car, but want the defects put right (breach of contract), or a refund to reflect the difference in value of the car you contracted to buy and the car you were sold (misrepresentation) write to the seller and outline what has gone wrong. It is often helpful (and persuasive!) to include a photocopy of any documents that support your claim. This might be in the form of an engineer's report, or garage estimate. If you get nowhere the next step is a 'letter before action' asking him to comply with your requests within a specified time-limit or be taken to court.

Chapter 2

Getting started

Learner drivers

Learner drivers must have attained the age of 17 and must obtain a provisional licence from the DVLA before sitting at the wheel. Any car driven by a learner must clearly display L-plates (and/or D plates in Wales). If a non-driving school vehicle is being used, the L-plates should be covered unless the learner is actually driving. At all times when driving, the learner must be supervised by someone who has held a full British licence for at least 3 years and is over 21. Note that breaches of these regulations may amount to the offence of 'driving otherwise than in accordance with a licence', even if no licence has been obtained. It is punishable by a fine of up to £1,000.

Where a licence could have been granted, unless there are 'special reasons' (see Chapter 4), disqualification is discretionary and endorsement (3-6 points) is obligatory.

It is also possible to commit an offence by allowing or causing another person to break the law (for example, lending your car to your 16-year-old daughter for a driving lesson on the road, supervised by her friend you know to be only 19).

Full licence

This may be obtained when a driver has passed the requisite DVLA test that contains a written theory test and driving exam.

Health and eyesight

A driver has a duty to report a health condition (or the prospect of such a condition developing) that might make his driving a source of danger to the public or to report certain prescribed medical conditions. This should be reported on the application form for a driving licence, or if such a condition develops after he has obtained his licence, at that later time. Failure to do so is an offence.

Similarly, to drive with uncorrected defective eyesight is an offence. An eye test forms part of the driving test, but there is an ongoing obligation to satisfy that test. A police officer who has reason to suspect that a driver has uncorrected defective eyesight may require him to undergo the test in the state that he was in when he drove (i.e. not wearing spectacles or wearing inadequately corrective ones).

Vehicle documents

The following documents must be obtained for all vehicles used (i.e. driven or parked) on a road:

- Excise licence ('tax disc') displayed on the windscreen.
- Test certificate ('MOT certificate') where the vehicle is 3 years old or more.
- Registration document issued by the DVLA, on purchase or transfer of the vehicle to you. This shows details of the registered owner, and the vehicle's specifications.

For details of offences relating to documentation see Chapter 4.

Insurance

Insurance is compulsory for the motorist. By law, everyone who drives a car, or an owner of a car who allows someone else to drive him or her in that car must have a valid insurance policy covering at least 'third party risks'. Many people have 'comprehensive cover' instead. It is an offence to use or drive the car, or to allow yourself to be driven in your car without valid insurance.

Third party cover

This means the insurance company will pay out compensation for damage caused to passengers or other road users caused by your negligent driving.

Comprehensive insurance cover

This usually means that in addition to third party cover, the insurance company will pay out for damage to your own car and personal injury to yourself. The policy may also cover your legal expenses, compensation for theft and the provision of a courtesy car. Remember, however, insurance policies vary and you must check to see exactly what you are covered for. Conditions may also apply. Common examples are cover limited to 'named drivers', cover only for social and domestic use of the car; and no cover for use on private land. If you drive whilst disqualified the insurance is automatically invalidated; you are thus committing two offences.

The Motor Insurers' Bureau (MIB)

All the motor insurance companies belong to this organisation. It pays compensation up to a maximum of £250,000 where:

a) You successfully sue a driver who had no insurance cover and cannot otherwise afford to pay the damages awarded to you.

b) In a 'hit and run' accident where the guilty driver cannot be traced and therefore cannot be taken to court. This is dealt with under the 'Untraced Drivers Agreement'. The Bureau investigates your claim and the circumstances of the incident and may make an award. You can appeal against their decision.

Seatbelts

The driver and all passengers must wear seatbelts if they are fitted to a car, both front and back. It is an offence not to do so and adult passengers will be held responsible for failures to comply. The driver will be held responsible in law for himself and any child passengers who are not complying (see below for the further requirements as to child passengers). The penalty for this offence is a £500 fine. It is possible to gain exemption from the seatbelt rules if, for example, you hold the relevant medical certificate.

Children

Children over the age of 12 or who are 1.5 metres or more in height may sit in the front passenger seat, but they must wear a seatbelt if one is fitted. Children between the ages of 3 and 12 (or under 1.5 metres tall) may sit in the front or back passenger seats but should wear an 'appropriate child restraint', or at least a seatbelt if fitted. Under 3s should wear the 'appropriate child restraint', whether in the back or the front of the vehicle.

An 'appropriate child restraint' means a baby carrier, or specially designed child seat appropriate to the child's size and weight.

If the child passengers are not conforming to these rules it is an offence for the driver (unless he has a reasonable excuse) to drive the vehicle. The penalties for this offence are as follows:

Child passenger in rear seat	£200 fine
Child passenger in front seat	£500 fine

Overloading

Passengers

It is an offence to 'use' a motor vehicle or trailer (including caravans) on the road when the number of passengers it carries, or the manner in which they are carried, results in the risk of injury to any person. Note that using a vehicle on the road includes parking it on the road, and even risk of injury to the passengers or the driver will count.

Loads

If a load is carried in or secured on a vehicle or trailer (including caravans) so that the weight, position or distribution of that load poses a danger of injury to any person an offence has been committed.

The maximum penalty (relating to domestic vehicles) for either of these overloading offences is £2,500, with discretionary disqualification and obligatory endorsement (3 points). See Chapter 4 for an explanation of how the penalty system works.

Caravans and camper-vans

A caravan is deemed to be a 'trailer' for the purposes of road traffic law in the UK. Lower speed limits apply when one is being towed:

Built up areas:	30mph
Single carriageways:	50mph
Dual carriageways:	60mph
Motorways:	60mph

Contact the RAC or AA for details on speed limits abroad.

A 'camper-van' or motor-caravan (up to 3.05 tonnes unladen) is subject to no separate speed restrictions.

It is an offence to allow a vehicle or trailer (i.e. caravan) to be on a road which poses a threat of injury to any person by virtue of its condition, load, carriage of passengers or the purpose for which it is being used.

Motorway driving

Driving on motorways in Britain is to a large extent the same as driving on any other road. The same offences can be committed on motorways, and a driver's liability for negligent driving is the same as described in previous chapters.

Drivers need to be aware of the particular skills required of motorway driving, given the higher speeds; infrequent interchanges and slip roads; different overtaking conditions; traffic control systems and (inevitably) roadworks. Refer to the Highway Code for further guidance.

Restrictions

Certain types of road users may not use motorways. These include pedestrians, provisional licence holders (learner drivers), some agricultural vehicles, horse-riders, pedal cycles and motorcycles of under 50cc capacity.

Vehicles pulling trailers and caravans are generally not permitted to travel in the right hand (offside) lane of a three-lane motorway. Note also that caravan or trailer-pulling vehicles have a maximum motorway speed limit of 60mph.

No vehicle may stop on the carriageway, central reservation or verge. U-turns are not permitted and stopping is only permitted on the hard shoulder in emergencies.

2

Chapter 3

Accidents and civil claims

Civil law exists alongside criminal law. The civil law provides for the party at fault to compensate the innocent party for loss and damage (i.e. the cost of repairing a damaged vehicle, or the value of a 'written off' one). Compensation for personal injury can also be ordered by a court; this will include sums for incidental expenses past and future and an amount representing 'pain, suffering and loss of amenity'.

The Criminal Justice System - criminal law - exists for the state to punish offenders. The police and the Crown Prosecution Service are responsible for gathering the evidence and prosecuting the offender.

In some circumstances, there will be overlap of civil and criminal law. For example, a driver involved in an accident may find himself prosecuted for careless driving (i.e. criminal proceedings) in the local Magistrates or Crown Court, and also be taken to the County Court or High Court by the other driver in a civil action for 'negligence' (i.e. civil proceedings).

Is someone at fault?

Every driver must drive with the 'ordinary care and skill' of a competent qualified driver. If a driver falls below this standard and causes damage or injury to another road user or nearby property he or she will be 'liable in negligence'.

Most accidents occur between two or more vehicles (cars, motorcycles buses, etc.). However, a motorist may be involved in an accident with a pedestrian, roadside property, animals or parked vehicles. Additionally, it may be possible for a passenger to claim against the driver of the vehicle he was in at the time of the accident, if that driver has been negligent. Whatever the situation, the motorist is expected to exercise the ordinary skill and care of a competent and qualified driver.

Common examples of liability:

- Veering or pulling out into the path of lane of another vehicle without adequate warning.

- Driving too fast for the road conditions and not being able to stop in time to avoid collision.
- Failing to keep a satisfactory look out for vehicles or other hazards.

Whether a driver will be found by a court to have fallen below the standard of driving expected of him depends on the circumstances of the case. Failure to observe the recommendations of the Highway Code can be used to show a driver was negligent. On the other hand, showing the court that the recommendations of the Highway Code were followed help to show the driver was not negligent

Contributory negligence

The law imposes a duty on every person to take reasonable care for his own safety. In circumstances where the victim of an accident is found to have been to some extent careless for his own safety the damages (compensation) are reduced accordingly. For example, a passenger sues the driver of a car whose negligent driving caused him to be seriously injured. However, his damages will be reduced by a percentage (up to one third) because he was not wearing a seat belt, and this contributed to the extent of his injuries.

Unavoidable accidents

Not every accident arises from the negligent driving of a motorist involved. A small number of accidents happen despite reasonable care being taken by the driver(s). Even if people are injured and property damaged, the law will not hold the driver(s) responsible for compensation in such a situation.

Accidents – what to do if you have one

Duty to exchange details

Do not leave the scene of the accident immediately. You must stop for a reasonable length of time to allow any interested party (the other driver or the owner of property or an animal damaged or injured), or a policeman to take your details.

Failure to (a) stop and/or (b) to give details if asked is an offence and carries a maximum penalty of 6 months' imprisonment; a fine of up to £5000; 5-10 penalty points or discretionary disqualification from driving.

The details required are:

a) Your name and address;

b) If you were driving someone else's vehicle, the name and address of the owner;

c) The identification marks of the vehicle (including the registration number);

d) If someone was injured, you must produce your insurance certificate; see 'Reporting the accident' below if you cannot produce it at this time.

Do not admit liability

It is sensible not to admit liability at the scene of the accident. Additionally, it is often a term of your insurance policy that no such admissions are made. You may be upset or angry, but questions of liability can be dealt with later. Even if you think you may have been at fault, later evidence might show that the other driver contributed to the accident, and this may affect the amount of compensation you or your insurers will have to pay. If any conversation does pass about who was at fault make a note of what was said by whom as soon as possible afterwards.

Take witnesses' details

If there is anyone who saw the accident and is prepared to be a witness or give a statement, take their name and address and tell them that you will contact them. Note that if you are successful, witnesses' travel costs and lost earnings for attending at court are recoverable under the Small Claims procedure.

The evidence of independent witnesses is stronger that non-independent witnesses, and eyewitnesses are more helpful than people who did not actually see the accident happen.

Example:

You are the driver of a red car and are involved in a collision with a blue car. Your passenger is WITNESS A: the driver of a yellow car is WITNESS B: and a pedestrian WITNESS C:

WITNESS A: "I was the passenger in the red car which was being driven by my best friend along the High Street at 25 mph. Suddenly the blue car shot out of a side road called Wellgreen Avenue. My friend did not have time to brake and the two cars collided."

This witness is not independent as he knows the driver of the red car, however, he saw the accident happen and can give useful information.

WITNESS B: "I was parked at a parking meter on the High Street 50 yards away from the junction of the High Street and Wellgreen Avenue. Suddenly I saw a red car coming towards me on the other side of the road at about 30 mph. Then I saw the blue car drive quickly out of Wellgreen Avenue directly into the path of the red car that did not have time to avoid the collision. The red car was shunted onto the other side of the road."

This witness is independent and an eyewitness. Her evidence is extremely helpful.

WITNESS C: " I was looking in a shop window on the High Street near the junction with Wellgreen Avenue. Out of the corner of my eye I noticed a red car drive along the High Street towards the junction. Seconds later I heard the screech of brakes and then a loud bang. I turned round and saw that the red car had collided with a blue car. When I got closer I saw that the blue car had shunted the red car right onto the other side of the High Street."

This independent witness did not see the accident occur, and therefore cannot give direct evidence as to which driver was at fault. However he can testify to the following facts: (i) which cars were involved, (ii) that one car at least tried to brake to avoid the accident, (iii) the position of the cars after the collision. All these factors may help a Court decide who was to blame.

Reporting the accident

Usually drivers stop and exchange details with each other after an accident. In that case there is no need to report the matter. If you have not exchanged details with someone who is likely to be affected by the accident (e.g. the owner of damaged property or a police officer attending at the scene) you must report the accident if:

a) any person (other than you) was injured, including passengers in your car; and/or

b) a domestic or farm animal was injured of killed (cats not included); and/or

c) property (other than your car) was damaged: this includes buildings/plants/trees adjoining the road, street furniture such as bollards and lamp posts, or another vehicle.

You must report the accident in person (a telephone call will not do) either to a police officer or at a police station at the earliest practicable time within 24 hours of the accident. Failure to do so is an offence. The maximum sentence is 6 months' imprisonment and/or a fine up to £5000. Disqualification from driving is possible, and the magistrates can endorse your licence with 5-10 points.

Note that if someone was injured and you did not produce your insurance certificate on request at the scene you must show it to the police

i) either when you report the accident or

ii) within 7 days of reporting the accident to the police

Failure to produce your insurance certificate is an offence that is punishable by a fine up to £1000. Note that the above duties are responsibilities imposed by the criminal justice system; they are unlikely to be relevant to a claim in the civil courts, and the civil courts will not punish a driver for failure to comply with the requirements.

Report the claim to your insurer

This may be a condition of your insurance contract, even if you do not intend to make a claim against your own insurers, or to ask your insurers to claim against the other driver. The insurer will tell you what cover you have.

The amount of compensation that can be claimed

The courts can order an unsuccessful defendant to pay the claimant a sum of money reflecting the loss he has suffered ('damages'). The aim is compensation of the claimant, not punishment of the defendant. Only certain types of loss can be claimed; these are known as 'heads of damage'. The following is a list of the most common heads of damage.

1) The cost of repairing a car or other property damaged in the accident. Where property would cost more to repair than its actual worth it is called 'beyond economic repair' or a 'write-off' and the write-off value is recoverable from the defendant, less any scrap value which the claimant should obtain by selling the car.

2) The costs incurred reasonably as a result of damage to property or injury

   e.g. the cost of using public transport or a hire car (if reasonable in the circumstances) whilst a car was off the road or being repaired,

   e.g. the cost of doctors' report fees, emergency treatment fees and prescriptions in a case of personal injury.

3) A sum representing loss of earnings and 'pain suffering and loss of amenity' in respect of a personal injury. The sum tries to represent compensation for the pain caused by the injury and the effect it has on the claimant's life. For example, an injury which causes a great deal of pain and requires long-term treatment, restricts the sufferer's ability to do the housework and prevents her from continuing her hobby of competitive windsurfing will require more compensation than an injury that needs minimal treatment, heals quickly, and does not stop the sufferer from working and living as normal after some initial discomfort. The Courts obtain guidance from compensation paid out in similar previous cases.

Negotiated settlements

It may be possible to avoid resorting to the court by parties coming to an agreement. This may happen at any stage; before court proceedings are issued; during the preparation for the hearing; at the door of the Court; or even during the trial before the judge gives judgment (though not in front of the judge!). Usually the defendant agrees to pay some or most of the claim, or pays the whole of it but pays no legal costs. However, each settlement depends on the facts of each case, and the bargaining position of each. There are considerable advantages for settling a dispute out of court:

The risks of litigation

If the case does not settle, the parties will have their evidence tested in court. There is always a chance that a claim or defence might not be proved. The weaker a party's evidence the riskier the litigation. This is particularly so in road traffic cases where there are independent witnesses and one driver's word is against the other's. It may be simpler and cheaper to settle before the case comes to court.

Compensation will be paid sooner

All court cases, even straightforward Small Claims cases, take time. Even if the court orders compensation there may be further delay of 'enforcing judgment' (i.e. actually obtaining payment of the damages).

Convenience

While some people will not be worried by the prospect of going to court or arbitration, many people will be nervous of having to give evidence, especially under cross examination. Additionally, the inevitable delay of court proceedings means that the prospect of going to court may be hanging over one for a period of months. Settlement shortens the delay and avoids the case having to come before the court.

It's not worth having your day in court

Remember, it is not worth going to court just to get an apology. If the offer is sensible, accept it. If you think that you will be ordered to pay compensation by a court, make a realistic offer at this stage.

Relying on criminal convictions

If one or more of the parties was convicted of a motoring offence related to the incident which is the subject of a civil claim, evidence of that conviction in the form of a certificate obtained from the convicting court can be placed before the judge. Such evidence will strengthen the case against the convicted person.

Challenging evidence of conviction

The evidence of conviction may be challenged at the civil hearing on one or more of the following grounds:

a) That alleged offender was not convicted as alleged. i.e. the wrong person, court or offence is cited on the certificate, or

b) That the alleged offender was wrongly convicted. Note that this will not overturn the conviction

c) The conviction is not relevant to issues in the civil case. i.e. it arose out of a separate incident.

Motoring offences

Chapter 4

A motorist may be accused of a motoring offence in the following situations:

At the roadside...

- warning from a police officer and no further action
- Fixed Penalty Ticket or Vehicle Defect Notice
- warning that prosecution is being considered
- arrest and questioning at a police station (available for only the most serious offences)

At home...

- receive 'Notice of Intention to Prosecute' and/or
- receive summons
- arrest on a warrant

Note: if you were arrested for committing an offence you will be either kept in custody (remand) until the next court session or will be 'remanded on bail'. The police can impose conditions of bail for example (to pay a 'security' to reside at a particular address or to report to a police station). If you are granted bail you must attend court at the correct time and on the correct day. Failure to do so is an offence called 'failing to surrender' that is punishable by up to 3 months' imprisonment, and/or a fine up to £5000.

Fixed Penalty Tickets

The Fixed Penalty Ticket system was set up to save the expense and delay of taking drivers to court for committing certain offences. The police officer offers the motorist a 'ticket' at the roadside. The motorist can accept it or reject it there and then. If he accepts it, what happens next will depend on whether he is being charged with an 'endorsable' or 'non-endorsable' offence (see below). If he rejects it, or having accepted the ticket at the roadside decides to challenge the accusation by sending off the slip asking for a hearing at the Magistrates Court, he will be sent a summons (see below).

Note: the Fixed Penalty System is discretionary and the police can choose to give a ticket or to prosecute the motorist through the courts. The system does not apply to many offences; see the table at Appendix 2.

Non-endorsable offences

Offences falling in this category are the less serious offences such as illegal parking and failure to display a tax disc ('excise licence'). Although you will have to pay a penalty within 21 days, currently £20 (£30 for illegal parking in London) no penalty points can be endorsed on your licence. This type of ticket may be affixed to your car if the driver is not present. Having accepted the ticket, the motorist can ask instead for the case to be heard in court by sending off the slip within the 21-day time limit.

Endorsable offences

These offences carry not only a penalty (currently £40) but also a mandatory number of penalty points that will be endorsed on your licence. The police officer at the scene will ask to see the motorist's licence and if the ticket is accepted will ask him to surrender the licence in return for a receipt. The licence will then be sent away to have the penalty points endorsed upon it, after which it will be returned. The penalty is payable within 21 days, but if the motorist wishes he may instead ask for the case to be heard in court by sending off the slip within the time limit.

If the motorist does not have his driving licence with him when asked to produce it by a police officer, he will be asked to produce it at a police station within the next seven days. Note that it is an offence not to comply. The police may then decide whether or not to offer him a ticket when he takes his licence to the police station.

Each offence has a specific number of penalty points (see Appendix 2). If a police officer, on examining the licence sees that endorsement for the particular offence would automatically disqualify a motorist under the 'totting-up system' (i.e. would take the total number of points endorsed on the licence in the last three years to 12 or more: see below) he cannot offer the driver a Fixed Penalty Ticket. The police will then send him a summons to attend court instead.

Failure to pay the penalty

The ticket gives details of how and where to pay the sum. If the driver does not pay the penalty within the 21-day time limit the police will register the failure as a fine with his local court. But beware, the sum registered is the penalty plus 50%. So not only is it more expensive to pay late, but the courts have various ways of enforcing payment of fines.

Vehicle Defect Notices

If your vehicle appears to breach regulations relating to maintenance (e.g. defective tyres or faulty lights) the police may give you a Vehicle Defect Notice requiring you to put the defect right. Failure to do so will result in a 'PG5 Notice' being placed on your vehicle. This invalidates your MOT certificate and makes it illegal to drive your car. Ignore these notices, and the motorist risks being served with a summons.

Summons

Unless the alleged offences are connected to an accident the police must:

a) warn the driver at the time of the offence that prosecution for an offence is being or will be considered OR

b) 'serve' (i.e. hand or post) a summons to the motorist within 14 days of the offence being allegedly committed OR

c) 'serve' (i.e. hand or post) a 'Notice of Intention to Prosecute' for the offence within 14 days of the offence being allegedly committed.It is up to the motorist to prove to the court that the police did not warn him of their intention to prosecute or serve the summons within time. If he so satisfies the court he cannot be convicted of the alleged offence.

Arrest

In some circumstances (usually depending on the offence that is alleged to have been committed) a prosecution for a motoring offence may start with the arrest of the motorist. Most commonly, this will happen when a police officer reasonably thinks a motorist who has taken a roadside breath test is 'over the limit'. Where a motorist has refused to take a breath test, an officer may arrest him if he reasonably suspects him to have alcohol in his body (slurring speech or breath smelling of alcohol will usually give the drink-driver away).

The police also have power to arrest a motorist at the roadside if they have a reasonable suspicion that he has been involved in one of the most serious driving offences, namely manslaughter, causing death by dangerous driving, causing death by careless driving whilst under the influence of drink or drugs and 'taking a vehicle without the owner's consent' (colloquially known as 'joy-riding').

Traffic Offences

All prosecutions for criminal offences begin in the Magistrates Court. The majority of cases remain there, with a few more serious cases being passed up ('committed') to the Crown Court to be dealt with there. Offences fall into three categories:

1) 'Summary only' offences; these make up the bulk of traffic offences, and can only be tried in the Magistrates Court.

2) 'Triable either way offences', such as dangerous driving, may be tried in either the Magistrates or Crown Court, depending on the seriousness of the individual case and whether the defendant requests trial by jury in the Crown Court.

3) 'Indictable only' offences are only triable in the Crown Court; only the most grave of the traffic offences fall into this category.

The prosecution must prove its case

The prosecution must prove all the elements of the offence against the defendant 'beyond reasonable doubt'. This means that the magistrate or jury must feel sure that the prosecution version of events is correct. And if they cannot, the defendant must be acquitted.

Defences

Even if, on the face of it, a driver has committed an offence he may have a defence. If the magistrate or jury decides that he has made out the defence (i.e. they are satisfied that his explanation is probably true), they must acquit him. It is possible to raise more than one defence to a charge.

Statutory defences

Sometimes a defence is 'built into' the definition of an offence. A good example is 'failing without reasonable excuse, to provide a specimen of breath when required to do so'. If the defendant satisfies the court that he had a 'reasonable excuse' he will be acquitted. The court decides what is reasonable.

Mechanical defect

This is a defence only to certain offences, for example dangerous driving, careless or inconsiderate driving, and pedestrian crossing offences. A defendant who gives evidence of a mechanical defect which he had been unaware of, and which he could not reasonably be expected to have been aware.

Duress of circumstances

This pompous legal phrase really means that the defendant was driven by the extreme emergency of the situation he found himself in to do something he would not otherwise have done, and so commit the offence. Basically, the law recognises that the driver was forced to commit the offence by the circumstances of the moment, and will therefore not punish him for it. Cases where the motorist successfully relied on this defence in the past include a man who drove recklessly in his attempt to escape of people trying to attack him; and a man who drove with excess alcohol in his body as far as was necessary to escape from the people chasing him. Another example might be where a motorist has to make a split-second decision between two evils and in choosing one commits an offence.

Automatism

This has nothing to do with robots! Where the motorist is rendered incapable, through no fault of his own, of consciously controlling his vehicle he will not be held liable for an offence he committed at the time. As examples of this are rare, the illustrations usually given are somewhat far-fetched, for example, being knocked unconscious by a stone or being attacked by a swarm of bees while at the wheel. However, this defence will also apply if the defendant at the time of the offence suffered an unexpected and unforeseeable stroke or epileptic fit. If such an illness is foreseeable and the driver failed to take precautions (i.e. by forgetting to take prescribed medication, or continuing to drive despite suffering warning signs of impending illness) this defence will not be available to him.

Specific offences

Dangerous driving

The prosecution must prove that the driver or motorcyclist drove on a road or in a public place 'dangerously', i.e. that his standard of driving fell far below that expected of a competent and careful driver. The Highway Code can be used in court to illustrate the standard expected of the 'competent and careful' driver. The offence can also be committed if the vehicle was driven when it was in such a bad or dangerous condition that it was obviously dangerous to drive it. 'Road' includes filter roads, pavements and any road to which the public have access.

Factors that may be considered dangerous driving include:

- driving at excessive speed
- driving on the wrong side of the road
- going through a red light

- forcing other drivers or pedestrians to take evasive action
- causing injury to persons or damage to property

If you are accused of this offence, the magistrates may decide that due to the seriousness of the allegations the case should be committed to the Crown Court for trial if you plead not guilty, or for sentence if you plead guilty. If they decide instead that it is suitable to be dealt with in the Magistrates Court you still have the option to choose a jury trial in the Crown Court.

The maximum sentence a Magistrates Court can pass is 6 months' imprisonment and/or a fine of up to £5000. For more serious cases the Crown Court can punish by up to 2 years' imprisonment In addition, the driver will be disqualified (i.e. banned from driving) and must pass an extended driving test, unless there are 'special reasons'; his licence will also be endorsed with 3-11 penalty points.

Careless driving

This offence is committed by someone who drives a motor vehicle on a road or in a public place

a) without due care and attention or

b) without reasonable consideration for other road users.

This is self-explanatory, and the difference between careless (or inconsiderate) driving and 'dangerous' driving is one of degree. Again, failure to observe the Highway Code can be used by the prosecution as evidence of carelessness.

Factors that might be considered 'careless' or 'inconsiderate' driving include (although depending on the circumstances these may also constitute dangerous driving):

- overtaking on the nearside lane (ie 'under'-taking)
- tailgating
- emerging from a side road into the path of a vehicle or pedestrian
- being distracted by mobile telephone or passengers/tuning radio/ reading map
- causing a minor accident
- failing to keep a good look out for hazards

This offence will almost always be dealt with by the Magistrates Court. It is currently punishable by a fine of up to £2,500. You may be banned from driving for a period depending on how seriously the magistrates consider the offence. Your driving licence will be endorsed with penalty points unless you can prove there are 'special reasons' why they should not The points will reflect the seriousness of the offence, with a minimum of 3 and a maximum of 9.

Drink-driving offences

There are four principal offences:

1. Driving with excess alcohol
2. Driving etc. whilst unfit to do so through drink or drugs
3. Failing to provide a 'sample' of breath (roadside breath test)
4. Failing to provide a 'specimen' of breath, blood or urine.

Driving with excess alcohol

This offence is committed by driving, or attempting to drive, or being in charge of a motor vehicle on a road or public place whilst the alcohol in your breath, blood or urine is 'over the limit'. The limits are:

- 35 microgrammes of alcohol in 100ml of breath; or
- 80 milligrammes of alcohol in 100ml of blood; or
- 107 milligrammes of alcohol in 100ml of urine.

'Being in charge' means what it says: it includes a person who is in 'control' of the vehicle and is intending to drive it away, even if he or she is not sitting in the vehicle.

Examples

Mr Green has been drinking all evening. He is just leaving the pub intending to go to his car which is parked outside and drive home when he is arrested The keys are in his hand. This man is 'in charge' of the vehicle.

Mr Blue has been drinking all evening. He is just leaving the pub when he is arrested. He explains that he is waiting for the taxi he just ordered to take him home, and that he gave his car keys to the barman. This man is not 'in charge' of the vehicle!

How do the police test for alcohol concentration?

A police officer who reasonably suspects that a driver

a) has alcohol in his or her body

b) has committed a traffic offence while the vehicle is in motion

c) has been involved in a motoring accident

can require him or her to take a roadside breath test. Failure to do so 'without reasonable excuse' is an offence (see below). If the test is positive, or if you have refused to take one you will be arrested or asked to go to the police station.

At the police station you will be asked to take two breath tests on an approved device. The machine will produce a printout showing your name, the time and the date and the two readings. This will be used as evidence – though the Court will only take account of the lower reading. If for medical reasons the police decide that a breath test is not suitable, or suspect that the machine is not working properly they may require you to give a blood or urine sample. A blood sample must be taken by a doctor, and with your permission. Remember, refusal to give a sample without reasonable excuse is an offence.

If your breath test produces a reading of between 35 to 50 microgrammes in 100 millilitres of breath you must be offered the chance to replace the specimen with one of blood or urine, which if given will be used instead.

You will be given a printout of the readings or half of the blood or urine sample (so that you can send it away to a laboratory for analysis if you wish challenge the police evidence).

Sentencing drink driving offences

A conviction for 'driving' or 'attempting to drive' whilst over the limit carries a maximum punishment of 6 months' imprisonment and/or a fine of up to £5,000. You will be banned from driving for at least 1 year and have your licence endorsed with 3-11 penalty points (unless you can prove there are 'special reasons' why the court should not do so).

Being in charge whilst over the limit carries a maximum punishment of up to 3 months' imprisonment and /or a fine of up to £2,500. You may be disqualified from driving, and your licence will be endorsed with 10 penalty points (unless there are 'special reasons').

If the driver has a reading of 100 mg of alcohol or more in 100ml of breath there is a significant risk that the Magistrates will impose a sentence of imprisonment

Failing to take a breath test

This offence is self-explanatory; the motorist has refused without reasonable excuse to take a roadside breath test when asked to by a constable in uniform. You may also commit it if you simply 'fail' to take the test, which means that for example you have not given a large enough sample for the device to work. See below for what constitutes a 'reasonable excuse'.

The maximum punishment for this offence is a fine currently up to £1000. Your licence will be endorsed with 4 penalty points (unless there are 'special reasons' – see below) and the Magistrates may disqualify the driver (i.e. ban from driving for a certain period)

Failing to give a specimen of breath, blood or urine

This offence is committed when you fail without reasonable excuse to give a specimen of breath, blood or urine for analysis. See below for what the court considers as a 'reasonable excuse'.

Where the driver had been driving or attempting to drive the Magistrates can impose a maximum penalty of 6 months' imprisonment and/or a fine up to £5,000. The motorist will be disqualified for at least one year, and his or her licence will be endorsed with between 3-11 penalty points unless there are 'special reasons'.

Where the driver had 'been in charge' of the vehicle (see above) the maximum penalties are up to 3 months' imprisonment and/or a fine of up to £2,500. The licence must be endorsed with 10 penalty points unless there are 'special reasons'. The magistrates can also disqualify the driver.

What is a 'reasonable excuse'?

As a general rule only medical reasons (physical or mental) will be accepted (e.g. a chest complaint, or blood disease).The defendant should call his doctor as a witness to give evidence that he had a particular complaint at the time, and that the complaint rendered him unable to produce the relevant specimen or take the test, or that taking the test would have been injurious to your health.

Speeding

Driving in excess of the speed limit for that particular road can be dealt with either by a Fixed Penalty Ticket or by summons in Court. Remember also that some types of vehicle may be subject to speed restrictions, no matter what the speed limit of the road (e.g. cars pulling caravans or trailers).

Evidence

You cannot be convicted on the opinion of one policeman (or other witness) alone. Drivers are usually convicted on the evidence of

a) the evidence of two witnesses who both saw you speeding on the same occasion

b) one witness and the supporting evidence of a stop watch, Vascar gun, radar meter or speedometer

c) evidence produced by a speed camera of an approved type.

The speed limit

Most roads will have signs and 'repeater signs' to tell you what the speed limit is, but remember that where the street lamps are placed 200 yards or less apart the limit is 30 mph. The authorities may impose temporary or permanent restrictions on roads, and breach of these will constitute an offence. Remember that each incident of speeding is a separate offence.

UK speed limits

Type of vehicle	Built-up areas	Single carriageways	Dual carriageways	Motorways
Cars	30mph	60mph	70mph	70mph
Cars towing caravans or trailers	30mph	50mph	60mph	60mph
Buses and coaches	30mph	50mph	60mph	70mph
Goods vehicles (under 7.5 tonnes)	30mph	50mph	60mph	70mph
Goods vehicles (over 7.5 tonnes)	30mph	40mph	50mph	60mph

Defences to charges of speeding

If you wish to challenge the charge you must refuse a Fixed Penalty Ticket and ask for your case to go to the Court where you should plead not guilty.

It is, of course, no defence to say 'I didn't see the sign', as the law expects the careful and competent motorist to look out for and obey all traffic signs. However, if there was no traffic sign marking the speed limit (for example if it had fallen down or been taken away) or the speed sign did not comply with the regulations as to colour size and shape the motorist, it seems, has a defence.

Challenging the evidence of speed cameras, Vascar, radar guns etc

The prosecution must prove that the photograph or readout was produced by an 'appropriate device' and also must produce a certificate signed by a police officer explaining how the photograph or readout was produced. In addition, the prosecution may not use a photograph or readout produced by a device unless they have sent you a copy of it at least seven days before the hearing or trial.

Requirements to produce documents

If a police officer believes you:

a) are driving a motor vehicle on a road or

b) were driving a motor vehicle which was involved in an accident or

c) committed a motoring offence

4

he can ask you to produce your driving licence, insurance certificate or MOT certificate. It is an offence not to do so. However it is a defence to produce the required documents at a police station (of your choosing) within 7 days. Usually the police will issue you with an 'HORT 1' form which requires you to do so. If not, you will have to remember yourself. If required to produce your licence you must do so in person; other documents can be sent by post.

If you cannot produce the documents within the 7-day time limit you will not be convicted if you can satisfy a court that you produced them at a police station 'as soon as reasonably practicable' (see below). If you have not been able to produce the required documents at a police station by the date that the police asked the Court to issue a summons, you will have to satisfy the Court that it was not 'reasonably practicable' to do so. Acceptable excuses for not producing the documents in time might be that you left the country or were admitted to hospital for a period before you could go to the police station. You will need to back this up with documentary or witness evidence.

The maximum punishment for these offences is (currently) a fine up to £1000. Magistrates tend to consider this type of offence serious, because the law gives the driver so many chances to produce his or her documents.

Non-valid documents

The principal offences are using a motor vehicle on a road

a) without a current valid insurance policy or

b) without a current valid excise licence (tax disc) or

c) without a current valid test certificate (MOT certificate) if required.

'Using a motor vehicle on a road' means more than driving it. A vehicle parked on the road (even if it is incapable of being driven), or a car being towed is considered to be 'used'. This offence can be committed by someone who was not even driving; a person who 'causes' or 'permits' another person to 'use' the vehicle on the road without valid documents is also guilty of this offence. Of course, if another person was acting without your permission or knowledge you have a defence as long as you have not 'used' the vehicle yourself.

To avoid conviction you must prove that either you did not 'use' the vehicle, or you did not cause or permit another person to 'use' it or that you did have valid documents. Produce the documents in court. The court will look to see if the document was valid at the time of the alleged offence, and if it was not you will be found guilty. See Appendix 3 for the maximum penalties.

Bicycle, motor cycle and moped offences

Bicycles

There are various offences that apply specifically to pedal cycles. For example it is an offence to ride on the footpath (pavement), as it is to ride dangerously, carelessly, inconsiderately, or under the influence of drink or drugs on a road or in a public place.

The maximum fines available are as follows:

Dangerous:	£2500
Careless:	£1000
Inconsiderate:	£1000
Unfit through drink or drugs:	£1000

The Highway Code contains useful extra information for cyclists, and do not forget that the rules of the road apply to cyclists as well as to other road users.

Motor cycles and mopeds

These are classed as motor vehicles and the offences that apply to car drivers may be committed also by motor cycle and moped users. By law motor cyclists must wear a safety helmet, as must pillion passengers. The penalty for being convicted for failing to wear a helmet is a fine (maximum £500). You may be offered a Fixed Penalty Ticket instead of prosecution through the Courts. Note that followers of the Sikh religion are exempted from the obligation to wear a safety helmet.

Sentencing

There are three elements to the structure of a punishment for a road traffic offence:

1. A penalty for the offence (fine, imprisonment etc.)

2. A penalty in relation to the driving licence (disqualification, penalty points)

3. Other orders such as compensation for property damage or personal injury, or a contribution to prosecution costs.

These are discussed in turn below. Together they make up the sentence, but a sentence will not necessarily be composed of all of these types of orders. The Tables in Appendices 1, 2 and 3 describe the maximum penalty available for some of the most common offences.

Types of penalty

Absolute discharge

This is where the court orders no penalty for the offence (although it may be combined with 'driving licence' penalties or compensation orders) and cost orders.

Conditional discharge

The court imposes no penalty for the offence (although it might impose a 'driving licence penalty' or 'other order'; see below) . However, the court will also specify a period and if the offender commits any new offence within that period he will be re-sentenced for the original offence by the court dealing with the new offence.

Fines

This is self-explanatory. The amount of the fine will reflect the seriousness of the offence and the means of the offender. The court may accept an offer by the offender to pay in instalments and usually a weekly amount will be fixed. Payment is made to the fines office of the Magistrates Court imposing the sentence. However you could ask the magistrates to transfer payment to a more convenient Magistrates Court.

Community penalty

This category includes 'probation order' and community service orders. A probation order requires the offender to submit to the supervision of a probation officer for a period time (between 6 months and 3 years) There may be a condition to attend a drug or alcohol dependency programme. Proposals for such supervision will be contained in the 'pre-sentence report' prepared by the probation service.

Community service orders require the offender to spend a specified number of hours doing unpaid work in the community. The probation service supervises such an order, and will have considered the suitability of the offender and the availability of projects in a pre-sentence report.

It is also possible to combine both probation and community service order (called a 'combination order').

Imprisonment or other forms of custody

This penalty is self-explanatory. The maximum length of imprisonment for selected offences is shown in the Tables at Appendices 1 and 2

This will be imposed where the Court thinks the offence(s) is so serious that only custody can be justified. It is very rare for the maximum term to be imposed.

Licence-related penalties

Disqualification from driving

Some offences provide for the immediate disqualification from driving. The court may have a discretion to disqualify but for some offences they must disqualify ('obligatory immediate disqualification').

The other circumstance in which the court must disqualify a driver is when a licence is endorsed with 12 or more penalty points during a three-year period (the 'totting-up procedure'). See also the new regime for totting up points by newly-qualified drivers below.

Obligatory immediate disqualification

The magistrates or Crown Court must disqualify the driver for at least a minimum period unless there are 'special reasons' not to do so (see below). The minimum periods are:

(i) at least 12 months or

(ii) at least two years where the driver is convicted of manslaughter, 'causing death by dangerous driving', or 'causing death by careless driving whilst under the influence of drink or drugs', having previously been disqualified for 56 days or more in the last three years; or

(iii) at least three years where the driver is convicted of 'causing death by careless driving whilst unfit through drink or drugs', or drink driving, or failing to provide a specimen plus an obligatory disqualification offence, having previously been convicted of any of these offences within the last 10 years.

Offenders convicted of drink-driving offences may be offered a reduced period of disqualification for attendance on a course designed to address the problems and behaviour of drink-drivers. It is up to the offender to pay for such a course; the Court should inform him what they are at the time of sentencing. The offender must consent to the proposal before the Court can order it. Unfortunately courses are not available all over the country. Usually the pre-sentence report (see below) will inform the Court as to the availability of such a course in the locality.

Discretionary immediate disqualification

This is where the court, taking into account the circumstances of the offence and offender decides that disqualification is appropriate punishment. There are no maximum and minimum periods of disqualification.

Penalty points and disqualification under the 'totting-up' procedure

If the offence carries penalty points (see the Tables of Offences at Appendices 1–3) the driving licence will be endorsed by the Court unless:

(i) the Court disqualifies the driver for that particular offence (obligatory or discretionary immediate disqualification, as above); or

(ii) more than one 'endorseable' offence has been committed on the occasion in question, in which case only the penalty points relating to the offence which was given the highest number of points are endorsed;

(iii) there are 'special reasons' (see below).

How many points are endorsed?

Each point-carrying offence incurs either a fixed number of points or a number decided by the magistrates within a range to reflect the seriousness of the offence.

The totting up system

The Court then adds up the points endorsed on the licence within the last 3 years (or since the last totted-up disqualification if less than 3 years ago). If the number of points totted up is 12 or more (see below for the rules relating to newly-qualified drivers) the offender will be disqualified for:

(i) at least 6 months, or

(ii) at least 1 year if the driver has previously received a disqualification of 56 days or more in the last 3 years, or

(iii) at least 2 years if the driver has previously received two or more disqualifications each of 56 days or more in the last 3 years.

The only way to avoid such a disqualification is for the Court to find that there are mitigating grounds that merit a shorter period of disqualification or none at all (for example 'exceptional hardship').

Newly-qualified drivers

In the first two years after passing a driving test a driver is 'newly-qualified'. If the number of points accumulated during this period is 6 or more the offender's driving licence will be revoked and he or she must undergo a retest in order to obtain a new full driving licence.

'Special reasons'

If a court is satisfied that there are special reasons it need not disqualify an offender or endorse a licence notwithstanding such disqualification or endorsement is 'compulsory'. There is a very narrow definition of 'special reasons'. It means a circumstance or feature of the offence, rather than a circumstance relating to the offender. The following may qualify as special reasons:

- Drinks laced with alcohol without the Defendant's knowledge
- Driving with excess alcohol/at excessive speeds in an emergency

Parking

Chapter 5

Off-street Parking

This is provided by Local Authorities or private firms licensed by the Local Authority. Most of these will have ticket machines or payment kiosks.

On-street parking

Metered

This is provided by Local Authorities, who designate areas and impose restrictions (e.g. limiting the time allowed, limiting use to certain categories of person or vehicle). Parking meters require you to pay an 'initial charge', and an 'excess charge' if you stay longer than you paid for.

Usually road markings show the parking spaces but do remember to read the sign posts, which will tell you of the restrictions in force. If an area is 'designated' by the Authorities the restrictions are not lifted by the suspension of a parking meter. Therefore, if you park at a meter that is covered by a bag or other notice you may still be committing an offence if you park there, depending on the wording of the relevant designation order. Copies of the designation Order are available from the police or Local Authority.

The law is strictly enforced and it is no defence that you had to 'run and get change for the meter' etc. Often meters or ticket machines only operate during certain hours, so read the signs telling you about the restrictions and charges.

Permit system

These schemes are also run by Local Authorities which may limit parking to certain categories of vehicles or persons (e.g. 'residents only'). Note the permit system may not operate all the time (e.g. non-permit holders may be able to park in these places at certain times). As before, watch out for signs that tell you about the restrictions.

Yellow lines

Double

These mean that you cannot wait or park on that particular stretch of road at any time.

Single

These mean that you can only wait or park at permitted times. Look out for signposts that tell you what the prohibited times are.

Remember that there may be 'no waiting' or 'no stopping' signs signs marking the entry onto a stretch of road to which restrictions apply. Watch out for them, as yellow lines are only a guide. However, if the signs are not there or do not comply with the regulations you may have a defence.

Red Routes

These are designated 'priority routes' in London designed to keep traffic flowing. They are patrolled by the police.

Who is responsible for the parked vehicle?

The person who last drove the car (i.e. the person who parked the vehicle) is legally responsible for complying with any regulations in force.

> *Example*
>
> Mr A drives into town and finds a parking space at a meter. He has arranged that his wife will pick the car up and drive it home, using the spare set of keys. He places coins in the meter, but Mrs A is delayed by a telephone call and arrives late to collect the car. Mr A is the person who is legally responsible for the excess charge incurred.

What to do if you get a parking ticket?

Excess Charge Notice

The notice will give you details of how much is owing and how you can pay it. Failure to pay the excess charge in time is an offence punishable by a fine (maximum £500). If you have committed this offence whilst using a 'disabled-only' space without being an orange badge-holder yourself the maximum fine is £1000 (see below). As well as the fine, the unpaid excess charge will also be payable.

Fixed Penalty Notice

This will be offered as an alternative to receiving a Court Summons when a police officer or traffic warden considers you have committed an offence; for example unpermitted parking on yellow lines; breaching regulations for on- or off-street parking places. The Notice will be handed to you, or can be affixed to the windscreen of your vehicle. The penalty payable for parking offences is:

Illegal parking on a Red Route	£40
Illegal parking in London	£30
Illegal parking elsewhere	£20

On receiving a Fixed Penalty Notice you have the following choices:

1. Pay the charge immediately to the clerk of the relevant Court;
2. Request that the magistrates hear the matter, and plead 'not guilty'
3. Do nothing, and wait for the police to send you a further Notice (requesting payment of the penalty or information as to who is the owner of the vehicle) – if this Notice is ignored the Police will register the penalty as a fine at the Court. The amount of such a fine is 50% above the Fixed Penalty. The Court will then start 'fine enforcement proceedings' and will fix a hearing for you to appear before the Magistrates.

See the Appendix for table of parking offences and penalties.

Clamping

The police and authorised persons may clamp ('immobilised') vehicles that are illegally parked. They also have the power to move your vehicle to another part of the road, or another road altogether, and then clamp it. However, if your vehicle is at an on-street parking meter where the initial charge was paid up you cannot be clamped unless 2 hours (15 minutes in London) have elapsed from the end of the period paid for. Disabled orange-badge holders are exempt from being clamped.

A notice will be fixed to the vehicle telling you how to get it released. Not surprisingly, a charge is payable. Currently that charge is £38. Note that it is an offence to interfere with the clamping device, or the notice.

Private wheelclamping

The current law on 'private' wheel clamping is not clear. Some cases recently have described how vehicle owners parked on 'private land' (i.e. not a highway or authorised car park) and have been charged very high release and storage fees. Without clear guidance on whether this is lawful from the Courts the wisest measure is to avoid such parking places. Do not park where you are not authorised to do so. If there are clear warning signs to motorists on the private land that unauthorised cars will be clamped you are deemed to have consented to run the risk of being clamped if you are parked there without authorisation. Note in Scotland such private clamping is considered extortion and theft and is therefore not lawful.

Towing away

The Authorities may remove vehicles that are parked illegally, obstructively or dangerously on a road, or seem to have been abandoned. The vehicle may be moved to another part of the road or removed to a place of custody. In order to recover your vehicle you must satisfy the authorities that you are the owner of the vehicle and pay the various sums charged;

a) storage (at a daily rate)

b) removal fee

c) a penalty may also be payable in Greater London.

This can work out very expensive. If there has been a mistake for some reason you will have the chance to make representations to the authorities and ultimately to the Parking Adjudicator. If you are successful you may get any sums you have paid out refunded.

Disabled drivers

If you hold an 'orange badge' issued by the Local Authority you will be exempt from certain restrictions applying to on-street parking (and may be exempt from some restrictions applying to off-street parking). There is no charge or time limit for on-street metered parking places. Where there is a 'limited waiting order' there is no time limit, however in a 'No Wait' zone the limit is three hours and you must display the time disc correctly.

Nuisance and the motorist

Chapter 6

Road rage

'Road rage' is a term that has come into general use in recent years to describe aggressive driving or other behaviour in motorists directed towards other road users.

Common examples of types of road rage include:

- tailgating (driving very close to the car in front)
- flashing headlights
- hooting
- making offensive gestures
- verbal abuse
- physical assault
- chasing

Such behaviour tends to be directed to another driver or road user in order to intimidate or 'punish' him or her. However deserved such behaviour may seem to be, it is inexcusable and in criminal proceedings will be seen to be an aggravating feature. It follows that road rage incidents will be considered as more serious by the courts than straightforward incidents of 'bad' or inattentive driving. More importantly, road rage can be extremely dangerous (e.g. tailgating or chasing).

What to do if you suffer a road rage incident

Of course, road rage covers a wide range of behaviour, from the minor and merely aggravating to the very dangerous. Obviously, in a very serious incident where an assault or accident occurs the emergency services will attend. In less serious cases it is open to you to report the matter to the police in the normal way. Remember that there is no offence of road rage as such, but that the other driver's behaviour may amount to one or more of the following criminal offences:

- dangerous driving
- careless driving

- inconsiderate driving
- assault, etc.

The most important thing to do is to keep calm and avoid reacting angrily and aggressively yourself. To do so inflates the situation and puts you and other road users in danger. Try not to take offensive behaviour personally. Most road rage incidents resolve as drivers move away from each other. Try not to be rattled by what has just happened; keep your attention on your own safe driving. If necessary drive to a safe place and take a break for a few minutes to recover your composure. Never take out your feelings on other drivers; by doing so you will be perpetuating road rage behaviour yourself.

An unfortunate minority of road users falls victim to more serious road rage incidents. If this happens to you try to keep calm and concentrate on driving to a safe place. Your priorities should be

a) to avoid being or seeming confrontational

b) to maximise your safety

The Automobile Association recommends the following steps:

- avoid making eye contact with your aggressor;
- do not attempt to accelerate or swerve suddenly;
- if you are being followed or the driver continues to hassle you, drive to the nearest police station or busy place to get help;
- lock your car doors and keep windows and sunroof only partly open;
- when stopped in traffic, leave enough space to pull out from behind the car in front of you;
- if anyone tries to get into your car, attract attention by sounding your horn or a personal alarm;
- do not be tempted to 'have a go' and do not carry any sort of weapon, which may provoke further anger and end up in the aggressor's hands.

Road rage and mitigation in the criminal courts

If you plead guilty to an incident characterised by road rage, or are found guilty after a trial you will have the chance to speak about the offence and your personal circumstances (mitigation).

Explain to the court what aroused your anger, and tell them of any steps you have taken to address your behaviour. Such steps might be:

- taken advice or counselling on anger-management;
- taken steps to address underlying problems e.g. stress or tiredness while driving;
- undertaken driving lessons to 'rectify' bad driving habits.

If you pleaded guilty:

- written an apology letter to the 'victim' (via the prosecution, police or court)

If you pleaded not guilty and were found guilty:

- apologise orally to the victim if he/she is in court, or if not express your intention to do so

Noise nuisance and the motorist

Car alarms, loud noise and music coming from vehicles may amount to a 'nuisance', i.e. interfering with the personal comfort of people living nearby. Your Local Authority has a duty to take reasonable steps to investigate a complaint, and if they believe the noise is a nuisance they will serve an 'abatement notice' on the person responsible.

An abatement notice can be affixed to the offending vehicle or given to the driver, (or the person who is the registered owner at the DVLA). It will require the 'responsible person' to stop the thing that is causing the nuisance or to take other specified steps within a certain time. To appeal against an abatement notice served on you can do so to a Magistrates Court within 21 days. To ignore the Notice and to not comply with its requirements is an offence. This can mean heavy penalties: a maximum fine of £5000 and a daily fine for each day the nuisance continues after conviction.

If the abatement notice has not been complied with the Local Authority may abate the nuisance itself i.e. by immobilising or removing alarms or other equipment, or even the car itself.

Another method of dealing with 'street nuisance' is to complain to the local Magistrates Court. Remember to keep a record of all the incidents of noise etc. You must give the defendant at least 3 days' notice (for a complaint about noise) or 21 days' notice (in the case of other nuisances) in writing of your intention to take proceedings in the Magistrates Court. If the defendant is convicted the Court may impose a fine of up to £5000 and require him or her to take steps to prevent the nuisance occurring again. The Court may also order that the complainant's costs are paid by the defendant.

Motoring abroad

Chapter 7

Your insurance company or car-hire company will be able to give you comprehensive advice about motoring abroad; however, the following is a general guide to what you must consider before you go.

Driving licences

1. **New photocard licence**; these have been introduced in line with other European photocard-style licences and are acceptable in all EU countries. They are not identity cards and cannot be used in the place of a passport.
2. **Old-style pink and green paper Full British Licence**; this is acceptable in all EU countries. In other countries an International Driving Permit may be necessary (see below).
3. **Old-style green paper Full British Licence**; this is accepted alone in most EU countries and Scandinavia. In Austria a further form of ID with a photograph is required, and in Italy, Portugal, Spain, an International Driving Permit is required. In other countries around the world an International Driving Permit may be necessary.
4. **International Driving Permit**; this is obtainable from the large motoring organisations (RAC and AA) for a small fee and is acceptable worldwide. Indeed, where a British driving licence is not acceptable (see above) an IDP is a necessity. It is also a useful form of general ID as it contains your photograph. It valid for one year.

Insurance

As in the UK, motor insurance (third party, fire and theft) is compulsory in the EU and other countries. It is very important to check with your insurer that you are covered for the country you will be driving in. It may be sensible to have a more comprehensive cover than the minimum legally required (covering your own expenses, such as the cost of repairs, legal expenses and alternative transport arrangements etc).

Proof of your Insurance cover should be carried with you. A Green Card (International Motor Insurance Certificate) is not compulsory in EU countries, but it is internationally recognised, and may be more readily understood where there is a language barrier. A Green Card can be obtained from your insurer on request.

Proof of ownership

When travelling abroad, make sure you take your V5 document. This is sent to you by the DVLA on registration. It proves that you are the registered owner and keeper of the vehicle. If yours is mislaid you can obtain a 'Certificate of Registration' from the nearest Registration Office for a small fee. If your vehicle is hired you need to obtain a 'vehicle of hire' certificate (VE 130) from the AA or RAC, proving that you have permission to take the vehicle from the UK. Check with your hire company for further details.

Other requirements

Before you drive abroad, especially if you are unfamiliar with driving conditions there, check if there are other compulsory requirements or restrictions. Your insurance company may be able to give you this information; otherwise the relevant embassy or tourist offices should be able to help.

Common compulsory requirements are:

- GB sticker
- First Aid kit
- Fire extinguisher
- Spare set of light bulbs
- Warning triangle.

European Motoring Regulations

Country	Minimum driving age	Licence Documents	Maximum speed limit Kph (Mph) Built up	Trunk Rd	Motorway	Blood-alcohol units	Compulsory equipment	Other
Austria	18	New style pink & green licence or old style green UK licence	50 (31)	100 (62)	130 (81)	0.08%	Warning Triangle, First Aid Kit, GB Sticker	seat belts must be worn, under 12s must use appropriate child seats in the front, a motorway tax sticker must be displayed on certain motorways
Belgium	18	Full UK licence	60 (37)	90 (56)	70-120 (43-57)	0.8%	Warning Triangle, GB Sticker	seat belts must be worn, no under 12s in the front seat unless there is no adequate room in the back
France	18	Full UK licence	50	90/110	130	0.08%	Warning Triangle, if your vehicle has no hazard lights, GB sticker	seat belts must be worn, under 10s must use child seats
Germany	17	Full UK licence	50 (31)	80 (50)	130 (81)	0.08%	Warning Triangle, GB sticker	seat belts must be worn, under 12s must use appropriate child seats in the front
Greece	18	Full UK licence	50	80 (31)	100 (50)	0.05% (62)	Warning Triangle, Fire Extinguishers, First Aid Kit, GB Stickers	no under 10s in the front seat,

Italy	18	New style pink & green licence or old style green licence and IDP	50 (31)	90 (56)	110/130 (68)/(81) (The lower speed limits applies to vehicles under 1100cc)	0.08%	Warning Triangle, GB sticker,	under 12s sitting in the front should be adequately restrained, seat belts must be worn
Ireland (Eire)	17	Full UK licence	(30)	(60)	(70)	0.08%	GB sticker	
Netherlands	18	Full UK licence	50 (31)	80 (50)	70*-120 (44)*-(74) *NB: compulsory minimum speed	0.05%	Warning Triangle, GB Sicker	No under 12s in the front seat, Seat belts must be worn
Spain	18	New style pink & green licence or old style green licence and IDP	50 (31)	90 (56)	120 (74)	0.08%	Set of replacement bulbs, GB sticker	under 12s sitting in the front should be adequately restrained, seat belts must be worn
Scandinavia	18 17 in Norway	Full UK licence	50 40 in Finland	60 70 in Sweden	110 90 in Norway	0.05% 0.02% in Sweden	Warning Triangle, (Denmark & Sweden)	headlights must be switched on when you drive at all times (Sweden & Norway), seat belts must be worn
Switzerland	18	Full UK licence	50	80 (31)	120 (50)	0.08% (74)	Warning Triangle, First Aid Kit, GB Sticker	seat belts must be worn in the front, Motorway tax sticker must be displayed if travelling on motorway, under 7s sitting in the front seat must be adequately restrained
Portugal	17	New style pink & green licence or old style green licence and IDP	50 (31)	90-100 (56-62)	120 (74)	0.05%	Warning Triangle, GB stickers	

Remember that speed limits will be different and usually expressed in kilometres per hour, and that maximum alcohol limits will vary from country to country. Laws governing the minimum age of the driver and the wearing of seat belts may also differ.

The table on the previous pages shows some of the characteristics of motoring laws in popular destinations in Europe.

What to do if you have an accident abroad

This Guide cannot give advice on the law in countries abroad. However, the advice to motorists remains the same as it would be for this country:

- exchange details with other parties involved
- obtain names and addresses of any witnesses
- take photographs or a video recording of the scene
- write down your recollection of what happened
- take down the details of any police officers or other authorities involved
- contact your insurer.

Another useful source of advice is the local British Embassy (or High Commission, depending on which country you are in). Additionally, major cities may have a British Consulate where practical help and advice may be sought (e.g. legal representation and translation services). These services will cost money, so the best course is to have obtained wide insurance cover prior to leaving on holiday.

Appendices

Appendix 1 Table of selected offences

	Where is it heard	Maximum sentence	Disqualification	Endorsement points	Other
Causing death by dangerous driving	Crown Court only	10 years' imprisonment and/or unlimited fine	Obligatory (minimum 2 years)	3-11	
Causing death by careless driving under the influence	Crown Court only	10 years' imprisonment and/or unlimited fine	Obligatory (minimum 2 years)	3-11	
Dangerous driving	Crown Court	2 years and/or unlimited fine	Obligatory (minimum 12 months)	3-11	
	or Magistrates	6 months and/or fine up to £5000	Obligatory (minimum 12 months)	3-11	
Careless or inconsiderate driving	Magistrates	Fine up to £5000	Discretionary	3-9	
Drink driving (being over the limit)	Magistrates	6 months and/or fine up to £5000	Obligatory (minimum 12 months)	3-11	
Driving – when unfit through drink/drugs	Magistrates	6 months or fine up to £5000	Obligatory (minimum 12 months)	3-11	
Being in charge when unfit through drink/drugs	Magistrates	3 months or fine up to £2,500	Discretionary	10	Can plead guilty by post
Refusing to take a breath test (roadside)	Magistrates	Fine up to £1000	Discretionary	4	
Refusing to give a specimen of breath, blood, or urine ('Driving')	Magistrates	6 months and/or fine of £1000	Obligatory (minimum 12 months)		
('Being in charge')	Magistrates	3 months and/or fine of £2500	Discretionary		
Driving whilst disqualified	Magistrates	6 months and/or fine up to £5000	Discretionary	6	
Using a car whilst uninsured	Magistrates	Fine up to £5000	Discretionary	6-8	Can plead guilty by post
Using a car without valid MOT	Magistrates	Fine up to £1000	—		Can plead guilty by post
Using a car without tax disc	Magistrates	Fine up to £1000 or 5 × tax amount	—		Can plead guilty by post
Speeding on a road	Magistrates	Fine up to £1000	Discretionary	3-6	Fixed Penalty Ticket. 3 pts + £40 fine
Speeding on motorway	Magistrates	Fine up to £2,500	Discretionary	3-6	Fixed Penalty Ticket. 3 pts + £40 fine
Failure to comply with a traffic sign	Endorsable: Magistrates	Fine up to £1000	Discretionary	3	Fixed Penalty 3 pts + £40
	Non-endorsable: Magistrates		Fine up to £1000	—	Fixed Penalty £20 fine

Appendix 2 Offences: failure to fulfil duties

	Where is it heard	Maximum sentence	Disqualification	Endorsement points	Other
After Accident – failure to stop	Magistrates	6 months and/or fine up to £5000	Discretionary	5-10	
– failure to give details	Magistrates	6 months and/or fine up to £5000	Discretionary	5-10	
Failure to report an accident	Magistrates	6 months and/or fine up to £5000	Discretionary	5-10	
Failure to produce insurance certificate/ MOT certificate	Magistrates	Fine up to £1000	—		Plead guilty by post
Failure to stop when required to by uniformed constable	Magistrates	Fine up to £1000			
Failure to give name or address where it is alleged you drove dangerously, carelessly or inconsiderately	Magistrates	Fine up to £1000			
Failure to produce driving licence when required	Magistrates	Fine up to £1000			

Appendix 3 Parking offences

Offence	Sentence	Fixed Penalty Ticket amount		Other
Parking on yellow lines	up to £1000	London Elsewhere	£30.00 £20.00	Towing away fee £105
Breach of regulations	up to £500	London Elsewhere	£30.00 £20.00	
Abuse of disabled parking spaces (on street)	up to £1000	London Elsewhere	£30.00 £20.00	
(off street)	up to £1000	Not applicable		
Failure to pay initial or excess charge	up to £500 + value of the parking charge	Not applicable		
Obstructing the highway	up to £1000	London Elsewhere	£30.00 £20.00	Towing away fee £105

NB: All these offences are non-endorsable, i.e. no penalty points are endorsed on the driving licence.

Index